JAN   2010

DISCARD

FCPL discards materials that are outdated
and in poor condition, in order to make
room for current, in-demand materials.
Underused materials are offered for
public sale

D1154380

Virginia
The Old Dominion

Marcia Amidon Lusted

PowerKiDS press™

New York

For my husband Greg, with love

Published in 2010 by The Rosen Publishing Group, Inc.
29 East 21st Street, New York, NY 10010

Copyright © 2010 by The Rosen Publishing Group, Inc.

All rights reserved. No part of this book may be reproduced in any form without permission in writing from the publisher, except by a reviewer.

First Edition

Editor: Nicole Pristash
Book Design: Greg Tucker
Photo Researcher: Jessica Gerweck

Photo Credits: Cover © Superstock/age fotostock; p. 5 © Matthew Borkoski/age fotostock; p. 7 Getty Images; p. 9 Hulton Archive/Getty Images; p. 11 © www.istockphoto.com/Newton Page; p. 13 © Paul A. Souders/Corbis; p. 15 by Mass Communication Specialist 2nd Class Joseph M. Buliavac/Released; p. 17 Richard Nowitz/Getty Images; pp. 19, 22 (dog), 22 (flag), 22 (bird), 22 (flower) Shutterstock.com; p. 22 (tree) Sam Abell/Gettty Images; p. 22 (Denny Hamlin) Jason Smith/Getty Images for NASCAR; p. 22 (Pocahontas) Three Lions/Getty Images; p. 22 (Thomas Jefferson) Stock Montage/Getty Images.

Library of Congress Cataloging-in-Publication Data

Lusted, Marcia Amidon.
  Virginia : the Old Dominion / Marcia Amidon Lusted. — 1st ed.
      p. cm. — (Our amazing states)
  Includes index.
  ISBN 978-1-4042-8123-3 (library binding) — ISBN 978-1-4358-3372-2 (pbk.) — ISBN 978-1-4358-3373-9 (6-pack)
  1. Virginia—Juvenile literature. I. Title.
  F226.3.L876 2010
  975.5—dc22

                                2009006233

Manufactured in the United States of America

Contents

Virginia

Which state is not the oldest in the United States but holds more history than most other states? Which state has the Pentagon, which is one of the world's biggest office buildings? That state is Virginia! Virginia is found on the eastern coast of the United States. North Carolina and Tennessee lie to the south, Maryland to the north, and West Virginia and Kentucky to the west. Washington, D.C., is just northwest of Virginia. The Atlantic Ocean is east.

Virginia's history goes back to 1607, when it became the first of England's 13 American **colonies**. Along with Ohio, Virginia is often called the mother of presidents because eight U.S. presidents are from Virginia.

4

Shown here is the Pentagon, in Arlington, Virginia. It houses many of the offices of the U.S. Department of Defense. About 23,000 people work there!

Settling in the New World

The first colony in America was built on Virginia's Roanoke Island in 1587. This colony was later left by the settlers, though, and no one knows what happened to them.

In 1607, another group of English people started a colony, near the James River, in Virginia. Even though they suffered from hunger and sickness, the colony of Jamestown lasted and became the first **permanent** colony in America.

Virginia's nickname is the Old Dominion. King Charles II gave Virginia this nickname because it stayed **loyal** to England during a time of war in that country in the mid-1600s.

This painting shows the building of the Jamestown settlement, near the James River in eastern Virginia.

Virginia and War

Virginia has played an important part in American history. An important battle of the **American Revolution** took place in Yorktown in 1781. The British **surrendered** and the war ended. George Washington would become the first U.S. president, and James Madison would help write the **Constitution**. Both men were from Virginia.

When the **Civil War** started in 1861, states that supported **slavery** wanted to separate from the United States and become the Confederate States of America. Richmond was the capital of the Confederacy. Robert E. Lee, from Virginia, led the Confederate army. The Confederates surrendered in Appomattox, and the war was over.

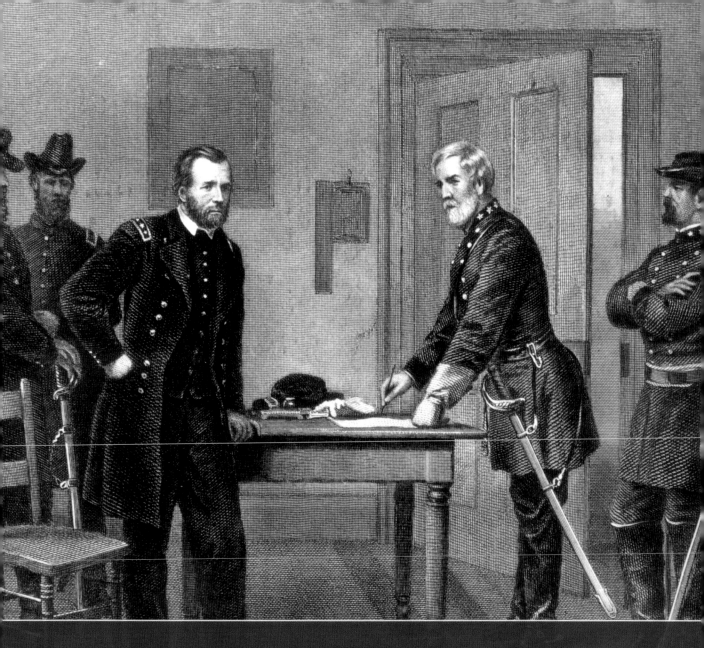

Robert E. Lee (right) surrendered to General Ulysses S. Grant (left) on April 9, 1865. This marked the end of the Civil War.

Mountains and Warm Weather

The land in Virginia slopes from the Blue Ridge and Allegheny mountains in the west to a flat, sandy area near Chesapeake Bay in the east. Chesapeake Bay is an estuary, an area where freshwater and salt water mix. It is 200 miles (322 km) long, and it has many kinds of plants, fish, and other animals living in it. In the northwestern part of Virginia is the Shenandoah Valley. "Shenandoah" comes from a Native American word that means "daughter of the stars."

Spring and fall in Virginia are warm, but summers can be hot. Winters do not get very cold, but it sometimes snows in the mountains.

The Blue Ridge Mountains got their name because they appear blue when seen from a distance.

What Lives in Virginia?

Virginia is home to many plants and animals. Almost two-thirds of the state is woodland, so trees are plentiful. The American dogwood tree, with its white flowers, is Virginia's state tree. Black bears, foxes, and coyotes are animals that live in Virginia's woodlands. Assateague Island, off the coast of Virginia, is famous for the hundreds of wild ponies that live there.

Virginia's state insect, or bug, is the eastern tiger swallowtail butterfly. This smart insect knows how to stay alive. When it is a caterpillar, it can make itself smell bad to keep enemies away. In some areas, the butterfly mimics, or copies, one of its **poisonous** relatives, the pipevine swallowtail.

Wild ponies have lived on Assateague Island since the 1600s. They travel the island feeding on grasses and a fruit called a persimmon.

Making More than Just History

Virginia is not just known for its historic sites. The state is also known for what is made and grown there. Factories in Virginia make car parts that are used to make cars in the state and across the country. In Newport News, ships are built for the U.S. Navy.

Virginia has many coal mines, too. It also has mines for several types of rock, including sandstone, limestone, and granite.

Fishermen catch crabs there that are then sold in many places. Farmers raise beef, cows, and chickens. Do you like potato chips? Farmers also grow potatoes in Virginia, and many of the potatoes are made into tasty chips!

The *USS Ronald Reagan*, shown here, is one of the many Navy ships built by Northrop Grumman, a company that builds ships in Newport News.

Exploring Richmond

Richmond is Virginia's capital city. The city has more than 200,000 people living there. Richmond has been called the city of churches because of the large number of churches in the area.

There are many things to do and see in Richmond. Richmond's **Canal** Walk follows several canals that were once used for travel. At the Meadow Farm **Museum**, visitors can see what it was like to live on a farm in the 1860s.

If you are looking for something fun to do in Richmond, you can explore the Virginia **Aviation** Museum. This museum displays airplanes from the past and present.

This is the Manchester Bridge, which crosses the James River and leads people into downtown Richmond.

A Step Back in Time

Williamsburg was the capital of Virginia during the American Revolution. Today, a part of Williamsburg, called Colonial Williamsburg, is a living-history museum. This means that the area looks as it did in the eighteenth century. Hundreds of buildings have been **restored**. People in **costumes** tell visitors about Williamsburg and what life was like there during that time. Visitors to Colonial Williamsburg can even learn how to dance the way people did in the eighteenth century!

Williamsburg's motto is "that the future may learn from the past." The city has been teaching people about America's past since 1926.

These actors in Colonial Williamsburg are dressed in costumes that are like the clothing people wore during the eighteenth century.

Virginia Is for Everyone!

Virginia is a great place to visit and live because it has so many different things to do. From the historic places, such as Jamestown and Williamsburg, to the wild ponies of Assateague Island, there are many interesting things to see.

You can go to the shipyards in Newport News and see some of the biggest ships in the world being built. In Charlottesville, you can visit Monticello. Monticello is the home of Thomas Jefferson, the third president of the United States. You can also drive across the Chesapeake Bay Bridge-Tunnel, the longest combined bridge and tunnel in the world. Virginia has something to offer everyone!

Glossary

American Revolution (uh-MER-uh-ken re-vuh-LOO-shun) Battles that soldiers from the colonies fought against Britain for freedom from 1775 to 1783.

aviation (ay-vee-AY-shun) The study and practice of flying.

canal (ka-NAL) A man-made waterway.

Civil War (SI-vul WOR) The war fought between the Northern and the Southern states of America from 1861 to 1865.

colonies (KAH-luh-neez) New places where people move that are still ruled by the leaders of the country from which they came.

Constitution (kon-stih-TOO-shun) The basic rules by which the United States is governed.

costumes (kos-TOOMZ) Clothes that make a person look like someone or something else.

loyal (LOY-ul) True to a person or an idea.

museum (myoo-ZEE-um) A place where art or historical pieces are kept for people to see.

permanent (PER-muh-nent) Lasting forever.

poisonous (POYZ-nus) Causing harm.

restored (rih-STORD) Put back or returned to an earlier state.

slavery (SLAY-vuh-ree) The system of one person "owning" another.

surrendered (suh-REN-derd) Gave up.

Virginia State Symbols

State Tree
American
Dogwood

State Dog
American
Foxhound

State Flag

State Bird
Cardinal

State Flower
American
Dogwood

State Seal

Famous People from Virginia

Pocahontas
(Around 1595–1617)
Born in the Tidewater
Region of Virginia
Princess of the
Powhatan Tribe

Thomas Jefferson
(1743–1826)
Born in Shadwell, VA
U.S. President

Denny Hamlin
(1980–)
Born in Chesterfield, VA
NASCAR Driver

Virginia State Map

Legend

⭘ Major City

★ Capital

〰 River

Potomac River

Arlington

Shenandoah Valley

Blue Ridge Mountains

Lake Anna

Charlottesville

Richmond ★

Chesapeake Bay

Atlantic Ocean

York River

Jamestown

Newport News

Virginia Beach

Norfolk

Roanoke

Smith Mountain Lake

John H. Kerr Reservoir

Allegheny Mountains

Virginia State Facts

Population: About 7,078,515

Area: 40,767 square miles (105,586 sq km)

Motto: "Thus always to tyrants"

Index

Web Sites

Due to the changing nature of Internet links, PowerKids Press has developed an online list of Web sites related to the subject of this book. This site is updated regularly. Please use this link to access the list:

www.powerkidslinks.com/amst/va/

24